GABRIEL'S

GW01418823

GABRIEL'S EXHIBITION

NEW POEMS

Stephen Gray

Mayibuye History and Literature Series No. 80

M
MAYIBUYE
BOOKS-UWC

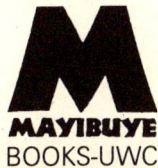

Published in 1998 in South Africa by
Mayibuye Books, University of the Western Cape,
Private Bag X17, Bellville 7535, South Africa.

Mayibuye Books is the publishing division of the Mayibuye
Centre at the University of the Western Cape. The Mayibuye
Centre is a pioneering project helping to recover areas of South
African history that have been neglected in the past. It also pro-
vides space for cultural creativity and expression in a way that
promotes the process of change and reconstruction in a democ-
ratic South Africa. The Mayibuye History and Literature Series is
part of this project. The series editors are Barry Feinberg and
André Odendaal.

ISBN 1-86808-378-0
Photograph of the author on back cover by Giovanni Giovannetti
Photograph on page 87 by Thelma Skotnes, taken in Nazareth in
1975.

Design and Typeset by **jon berndt Design**

PRINTED AND BOUND IN THE REPUBLIC OF SOUTH AFRICA BY
THE RUSTICA PRESS (Pty) LTD, NDABENI, WESTERN CAPE
D6323

ACKNOWLEDGMENTS

The first ten poems were begun while I was a fellow at the Hawthornden Castle International Retreat for Writers near Edinburgh, and most of those from 'Misadventures' to 'Ovid in his Exile' on a similar fellowship at the Rockefeller Foundation's Bellagio Study and Conference Centre, Lake Como - to these institutions and their personnel my gratitude.

Also to the editors of the following publications in which poems first appeared:

Ambit, London:

'Géricault's Shipwreck'

Ariel, Calgary:

'Sex and Drugs in the Caribbean', 'Fire on Sixth Avenue'

The Caribbean Writer, Kingshill, Saint Croix:

'Sex and Drugs in the Caribbean'

The English Academy Review, Johannesburg:

'Roots', 'Poppies', 'Commendation', 'The Anna Mary Letters', 'Child at Lake Como', 'The Martyrdom of Saint Sebastian', 'These Pigs Fly'

Equality, Johannesburg:

'These Pigs Fly'

Exile, Toronto:

'Poppies'

The Indiana Review, Bloomington:

'The Anna Mary Letters', 'Gabriel's Exhibition'

Kunapipi, Aarhus:

'The Anna Mary Letters', 'Symposium', 'Passages', 'South to South', 'Géricault's Shipwreck'

The London Review of Books, London:

'The Anna Mary Letters'

Matatu, Amsterdam:

'Sex and Drugs in the Caribbean'

Meanjin, Melbourne:

'Fireflies'

New Coin, Grahamstown:

'Symposium'

New Contrast, Cape Town:

'Sex and Drugs in the Caribbean', 'South to South', 'My Garden', 'Fireflies', 'Géricault's Shipwreck', 'C. V.', 'Passages', 'Marina Grande'

Scrutiny 2, Pretoria:

'Billets-Doux', 'Gabriel's Exhibition'

Southern African Review of Books, Cape Town:

'The Adoration of the Kings'

Staffrider, Johannesburg:

'Postcards', 'The Poet Laureate Saves the Rhino', 'Slaughtered Saints', 'Fire on Sixth Avenue', 'Modes of Transport', 'Ovid in his Exile'

Sunday Independent, Johannesburg:

'I. m. Olga Kirsch'

Wilfred Owen Newsletter, Shrewsbury:

'Poppies'.

Also the following books:

A Talent(ed) Digger, Hena Maes-Jelinek, Gordon Collier and Geoffrey V. Davis (eds.) (Amsterdam: Rodopi):

'Ovid in his Exile'

The Heart in Exile, Leon de Kock and Ian Tromp (eds.) (Johannesburg: Penguin):

'Slaughtered Saints'.

CONTENTS

ROOTS

I went back to my ancestral home
in that famous Borderlands,
from which the world was given some song
and the power of a pair of inky hands:

reivers the Grays, those minor thieves,
raiding the Chapmans and Livingstones,
Pringles in the djingles, Campbells in their shiels,
burnsing ballads over their dry bones;

last post before Hadrian's wall,
poets and Picts beyond the dung-ripe steep -
learned to use English better than the conqueror,
indistinguishable from their laird's sheep;

lowly; few stayed behind; exported people;
took, without reason, rhythm and their doodled rimes;
left croft and loch and falling steeple
to celebrate in metres their New Lits;

today it's jist as weel they emigrated;
the bus has run into a wave of caterpillars;
they'll eat the wheels, they're never sated;
more treacherous than all those Border Wars;

no more grass, the corn's uprooted
at the hairpin bend (First Pub in Scotland);
Guid God, laddie... This is worse than Rorke's Drift;
moths eat paper too and quills in my homeland!

POSTCARDS

I

X means a big hug
O stands for a deep kiss
Missing you; wish you were here
By Air Mail   First Class

II

Dear Public Enemy your rap
Rimes Apartheid with Nowhere to Hide
I hear ya 'nigger call' 'Nigga
Come 'n get me 'cause aam on ya side... '

III

Cheap Booze, Cheap Boys, pumped up
Steroid blonds, rough rear entry, rude
Sex *dirty* talk. What does a true Scot
Wear under his kilt? - a condom, prude...

IV

Went to my born church today I must confess
To view the meaning of the architecture,
The shaven congregation wore pink triangles,
No plaques for them, or for Gypsies and Jews.

V

I've joined the Anti-Nazi League
For 30p. my badge admits me to a die-in,
Add £1 to cover postal expense:
For a little more they disconnected the gas

VI

Don't let your children
Suffer your parents' crimes;
Recall: X O is no genetic code,
Means hug: kiss: hug: kiss: at all times.

POPPIES

You may not be forgiven
Those past horrors which poppies
In the seams of corduroy wheat
Bullet-holes of black
Splash red petals
Commemorate along the way

Never forgiven: these battlefields
Where men leapt from the copse
And spinneys piped up on
Rations of raw slave rum
To the metal hail of your
Harvesting machine-gun

There is no apology: behind the hedge
The fox palpitates at the
Gathering bark of dogs,
The thump of the rabbit,
Snake in a dovecot:
Man the killer comes.

Your cathedrals clank in memorials
To your glorious forgotten dead -
The long-knife people, buglers
And slaughterers, inches by blood,
Kill them as they clasp:
Not to forgive ever, ever.

There will be no forgiveness asked
For these scarlet flowers or given.

THE TROJAN HORSE

The beast I am fears neither bit, rein,
rod, spur or whip - I am heartless;
nor the riders I bear, not upon my back,
but huddled in my interior belly -
whispering brutes to burst out -
art wrought me this metal monster,
I care not for grass, corn, sugar-lumps;
a mare, I was born of no willing mother;
my father was armed, shot metal rivets;
the cream of a thousand ships - champions
of perpetual war - sneak out of my hold;
when honour fails, treachery will have to do...
sniffing smoke, I have raz'd a mortal town.

THE POET LAUREATE SAVES THE RHINO

Black one, built like a clad camper,
Horned in on the privileged feast -
Having served the royals his forceful gift
He turns to save the rhino, doomed beast.

Never has he seen one in its habitat,
Does not know they come in female and young too,
Exhibited in Venice in a velvet cage
Sprayed the masked courtiers in rhino-poo.

His libido of long dumb puritans
Mistakes the prick that grows between the quarters
For the instrument of self-defence upon the brow -
Ships the Zulus called them, masted in muddy waters.

Does not know how they go extinct -
With land, climate, language, wars and men
Lost… Africans must bite this bullet - meat,
Their debt to Europe - hack with more than a pen.

His manuscript at Sotheby's he'll raffle
With a lot of racial phobias besides,
Pray God he's the last of his kind now,
Rhinos are finer-tuned, know more of their rights.

UNTITLED

Some titles are better than the poems promised:
'After Lights-out' I used to plan on
And its companion, 'A Light in the Room.'

Recently I was going to do 'The Following Millennium':
Adjacent to the last scifi, 'Island off an Island.'
Inevitably 'Saving Grace', 'Birdcages
with Panoramic Wallpaper', 'The Story
on the Other Side', 'More Lights-out.'

Locally I've always meant to do:
'Stiff Competition at Sun City' and
'Kalahari Surfers Bite the Dust';
On file I still have: 'I'd Like to Help
You All in Your Struggle for Freedom' (famous song).

'Writers Do It between the Covers',
'Poets between the Lines', 'As if There
were no Tomorrow' for 'Those About to Die':
we salute you, we of 'Mule River',
'Not their Real Names.' 'And Now Read On.'

'Looks like You Bought the Good One, Brad… '
What about 'Personal Favours',
What about 'Dark Secret Life'?
But then, but then… I found the
Greatest title of them all (not mine):

'Sir Edward Elgar Hang-gliding
over Worcestershire' - without being
more tantalising… let's leave the matter
there.

COMMENDATION

Shall I compare thee?
beautiful number -
radiant as stained glass
the bruise upon your gloss,
collapsable sonnet
heav'nly lays -
shall I compare?
for thou art until kingdom come
and lesser mortals as well do
no less than hind and hock
magic key may unlock
the splendour falls
on castle walls,
feathery feathery, shall I?
tradesman and true
to British verse (back entrance)
a magic last minstrel's lay -
a summer day -
more, much more
the likes of which
words are nothing for
greater than
Shakespeare and Tennyson
no comparison.

THE ADORATION OF THE KINGS

by Jacopo Bassano (1510-92),
National Gallery of Scotland

Harder still; I bear gold from the Niger, lift to show,
These gifts from we three kings of old;
In their art I am doubletted in red
With buttons of pearl paler
Than this child who will burn in the light;
Whom these yeomen will let be killed,
A savage practice to be put down:
Crucifixion, their only image of love
As if this Mary thrown back in delivery
Were not enough suffering for one life;
Broken-columned ruins; fat pied horse;
Hunting dogs and grizzled donkeys.
Like animals themselves in winter they live
Entombed with the stink of these their creatures;
Infant mortality, the decay, the dirt.
Their lords are child-killers; the odds are
Any change he tries to make will kill him.
Their ghetto for Jews; where I come from
We do not have these discriminations.
Hardest of all in what follows:
I will be left out; for every one
Of Him my continent will bleed a million:
This is the cross we will have to carry.
But I was there, I was a witness and
I meant them to see, the silt washed,
The white-water stream tamed,

How these good aery grains of God
Could be there - soft; ductile; shiny; pure;
May be beaten to cover the whole world.

THE ANNA MARY LETTERS

To Hans Christian Andersen

I

Ulva Cottage
Hamilton
Scotland
1 Jan. 1869

Dear Mr Andersen, My name is Anna Mary,
Last-borne of Mary my mother, deceased
Of the desert fever while I was but a 'wee bairn';
I am but ten, too young to remember her voice.
I *do* like your fairy tales so much - the tin soldier and the ugly,
Ugly duckling. I would like to go and visit you;
When Papa comes home from Africa I intend
To ask him to take me. I live where he began
As a piecer of cotton, threading those bales…
Long enough to join us over six thousand miles;
What with the water-thrust and water-damp
The Clyde is perfect for the manufacture of cloth;
Without cotton my dolly'd have no clothes.
I'm sure he will agree. In the New Year.

II

17 June 1871

Four of his children in this cottage on the Clyde; good and damp
Enough to drive the cotton, even if it's not Victoria Falls.
I send you the photo of my Papa and me:
His arm is about me and mine about my dolly.

I would like you to notice my hoop-skirt and pantaloons,
But not my face and hair scooped away, ugly still;
Papa draws back breath and calls me 'sprightly' now;
If you ask me he's forgotten the meaning of his own hearth;
He says we're sickly and weak, bad seed,
But he's the one won't kiss for bad teeth, rotten tongue;
He was born here, he should know; we were born
In the wildest desert so generous, where a man may breath
                                                    indeed.

He said bright Denmark was out of the question:
Only dark Africa calls, where he may make himself
A paradise away from this, his woven, wet hell.

III

                                        24 Sept. 1874

O Hans Andersen, You will have seen from the papers
How the tale has no magic ending for us, *quack quack*.
My father is the one Mr Stanley found out there
And he could not persuade him to return to us.
Robert's gone, Thomas and Ossie too -
Poor seed, this little mermaid never will swim;
What great, great sorrow I have had this year.
I did expect Papa to take me to your Copenhagen.
Instead of going the different places I fully intended
With Papa, I have been obliged to take the sad journey to London
To see what's left of him buried in Westminster Abbey.
We had all wreaths of full white flowers
To lay on his coffin; our Queen sent one too
From out of her palace with deepest regrets.
I am the only one of our seed left alive now;

We shall be threadbare, me and my toy;
Don't you think flowers are so beautiful,
Ice-white and wound in a heart -
The shape of the continent where his lies?

IV

30 Oct. 1874

Back at our industrious Blantyre:
Papa's two most faithful servants were here last week
To visit me. Many interesting things they told
About Papa and one of them, called Chuma, made
A model grass hut in which he placed my doll
As an example, to show the position where
Father knelt and died; and Susi endlessly
Fussed with the bed to get it exactly correct.
Quack quack, my dear. What else can I say?
Susi says they brought his remains back from Ilala
Only to prove to the consul at Zanzibar no black man
Poisoned him; he died of his own disease. Tin god.
You're the one who understands
And I am your sincere friend.

SLAUGHTERED SAINTS

a row of graves in the veld, bar-code of death
at Sharpeville again - black coffins before
a soccer stadium of mourners -

this recurs as the great South African ceremony:
public weeping, no compensation, together
only in the mass shuffle of their united end

what then, once the chants and sermons are done,
the bodycount of liberation, the victims
guilty of their innocence, their reduction to dust?

who worked out how many it takes?
do they signify, either way?
- did anyone consult with *them?* -

the late martyrs of Boipatong - mother and babe
elbow to elbow in the winter grit - able-bodied
certainly had other hopes of their different lives -

and if they said they wished to speak to us
what then? and who would listen?
what would we offer in return for their few, honest words?

would they then set about to kill their killers?
mass with sticks and stones their dreadful regret,
rampage against their lack of fortune?

take by the throat the privileged few,
scoop from the mouths of others' children
a spoonful of porridge, a nub of meat on the bone?

this early death hath only made them hungry
for the life they never had: girlfriends,
fast cars, for shopping from huge supermarkets

and the greedy needs of the dead do not end:
they want impossibly: music and song,
they want padding and waterproof, comforts

next thing they'll want mod cons,
to watch themselves on TV getting mown down
by private armies, presidents of all

parties and demonstrations come to mourn them;
what they'll next demand is bullets
(just wait!) and their own rolled razor-wire,

keep the predators out, flowers on their tombs…
but no one asks the blood and ashes, nor ever will.
what would happen then would only overkill…

don't anyone consult with them; bury them,
the lonely martyrs of Boipatong,
lest the slaughtered saints recur, recur.

SEX AND DRUGS IN THE CARIBBEAN:
FERRY TO PORT ROYAL (1992)

From capital Kingston to an older drunk one sunk
Like Babylon in buccaneer, bounty days;
This dying splendour, is it really enough?
Scavenging the bay brown pelicans sort
The silver streak from greasy plastic,
Eject their shit on shore; tourists come
To Jamaica (the Tourist Board says) for sex and drugs;
Always did, for five hundred years.
'Columbus he lie, he lie, he lie,'
Says the calypso; for counter-discourse
This Jah Shaka turn- 'em-round reggae
Is exemplary: look how in love they are
With names like Windsor Palace, Ugly River, Nanny Town.
Columbus and their Empires lied, revered more
An Old Dying than a New World...
For one dollar down that mangrove cay
Is reached by the dead-pan poor, a dormitory
Of dreadtalk, the African Methodist Episcopal
Zion Church - talk of heaven Lord's on its way!
Not now, not today; sex and drugs we have
But Heaven He Delay... and their awful
Repercussions: rubble too large to sink again.
At the Historic Site where one-limbed Morgan, Nelson
Blew all other Europeans out, screwed
Their conquests to the flags, adjusted
By hurricane, quakes and flood, we land
On the stony palisades, a reef that stopped

Breathing a few months ago… and I know:
This has never been their place or mine:
Belongs to the deep redoubt and cannon-thrust.
'One Blood in One Beat,' says the painted
Crimson heart on the stall of another
Folk expression for my collection: Pearl's
Hi-way Takeaway and Creamy Café:
Stack the cone double, chocolate…
Fan my sweatband, this melting handful
Coolly to fellate: my protest against
The radiant greenhouse effect. The hotel
Like a compound - scenic prison - has a pool
The colour and tiled consistency of any,
The chemicals have been flown in, so has
The fruit, the veg, the steak, the prawns:
Salkey has written that's what independence
Meant: now even their white overproof rum
Is imported. All of this means:
For the small change that burdens
My money-bag those rickety children
Will dive deep and burst their tiny lungs,
After valueless coins these emaciates -
The tourist and the new slaves - we're down to
Clasping through blue leaves… parting the water
After flicks of silver… money more than
Air, money more than oxygen…
The haemorrhage of sacs… tissue…
Which is what we are down to: begging
For mere coins… under the sexy, druggy swell.

PADRAO

A stone
obelisk
confronts a continent
across burning sands
it came
by sea
as the known
to unknowable
man to stake
footholds for
a distant God
anthills are
Africa's ver-
sion of such
lone fingers
pointing unto
Him although
their life is
automatically
there while our symbol of
love is based on our pain

DARWIN'S CONTACT

Found this: 'In 1836
at Bantry Bay on the shoreline
Charles Darwin described these rocks
(discovered by Clarke Abel in 1818).
Some 600 million years ago
the molten white granite was forced up
into the sedimentary slate layers,
causing them to arch upwards
and break. An impressive
zone of dark slate with pale
intrusive granite, an inspiring
influence on the historical
development of geology. An example
of contact between a sedimentary
and an igneous rock.'

Checked it out: others meet here:
land and sea, couples at the take-away.
The fog-horn warns them all:
make contact, freeze, grip.

THE HEAD

To the head run the impulses of a subcontinent
    from across a far landscape of sea earth road
    highway lines of communication like a net
thrown in electronic circuits operating day long

the head is a hive of interrelated comings
    and goings where the quarters of a globe
    close into one masterly terminal radiating
and receiving the impulses of that whole subcontinent

the intensity of activity within the head is thus
    almost impossible to assess in its complexity
    the coming and going as in a beehive
hums with great organisation and the making of things

this coming together then is impressively magical
    you have to understand the co-operation
    of men and women of all types and sizes
within one whole before you can see how it works at all

the head is a symbol a storehouse and a home
    in a graded landscape cool as a tree
    growing from deep foundations upward
and outward in a rush of focal impulses like light.

NENUPHAR

Now, the gathering of bees
As my purple, my yellow
Breaks apart in air.
From mud, slime, the silt
This bursting beauty.
The flow, the flood, whereafter
I am transferred in light.

FIRE ON SIXTH AVENUE

A miner's semi not yet Delhified,
Firemen up ladders axeing the sink,
The domestic in a shrunken shift trying to hide
Her burning backyard bully in their candlewick,

While the Madam and her maan on the one-armed bandits
To Sun City are gone to reschedule their debts,
Should've rather, say my neighbour pandits,
Stayed home for once to hedge better their bets.

The fault's electrical, the sparks and spangles,
Burn of cordite and anthracite and corks,
From a brandbestryder's proud glove dangles
A cross-eyed kitten rescued from Guy Fawkes.

More smoke billows now from the radiator
Of the new red Brixton fire-engine, choked up,
Than from the wreck, the pump's more air than water,
A dog stands on the hose and the hose's all blocked up.

In groups we relish the scene, not yet new South Africans -
Areas of whites, of blacks, of Indians, of others.
Thank God we feel, as usual, the horror-stricken
Are someone else... we still prefer guns to brothers.

Consider that cat's view in this transition: it's not too late,
For rats the hotplate of pressed steel's the only solution,

Beneath the ozone layer's still air enough not to asphyxiate,
Some fires are just fire, not the full scale revolution.

Otherwise curl up the better to sleep it off, folks,
The decoder's stolen, insurance will just fork out,
With sirens Lakshmi's taken and the smoke's
Held in from a stompie, this time really crushed out.

This is a suburb of Cinderellas stuck in the ash,
Instead of chandeliers the well-wrought burglar-bars,
A Lubners three-piece showing its guts through the gash,
Look away, look up… the geyser steam rises to the stars.

MODES OF TRANSPORT

Once the problem was, ah once,
Did poets praise simply the veld and the vlei
Or (with which tongue) speak for the poor;
Now the question is: who gets their Porsche?
And blessed are the Ministers,
For they shall inherit the Merc.

Poets who adored priceless water and roofs,
Taught letters, numbers and trees,
Want air-time and royalties for which one of the few
Gets the air-conditioned BMW.
And blessed are the Ministers,
For they shall inherit the Merc.

In exile spent my years dictating lines,
Oral ones and party ones a million times,
Polishing my roots from Umbogintwini;
All I have polished now is my Lamborghini.
And blessed are the Ministers,
For they shall inherit the Merc.

On the tapedeck I hear myself
Singing the old blues, singing the old blues;
Cut out this Shakespeare, man, he was anti-jigaboo,
And fuck that Juliet, grab the Alfa, Romeo.
And blessed are the Ministers,
For they shall inherit the Merc.

The taxi wars cross my nation's map,
Guns and talents exceed the limit, go to scrap,
Mazda, Mitsubishi, do they do bullet-proof, alarms?
Camry and Stanza, a poem across my palm.
And blessed are the Ministers,
For they shall inherit the Merc.

We are driven cause we're voted for,
If we'd had more time we'd have published more,
Keep your Audis, Nissans, Peugeots, Jags,
Passing a donkey-cart, my heart goes to the mass,
And blessed are the Ministers,
For they shall inherit the Merc.

THESE PIGS FLY

If this keeps up - my friends and their last friends
dying of AIDS - I shall have to take steps:
study aerodynamics, grow wings to join them.
For this world as they leave is less worth clinging to,
where presidents brand them pigs, forbidden flesh
beyond their law, as in some old Jewish slander.
But out of their ash, behold! a vane, a quill, a crest:
these are the feathery chicks I never believed in.
They rise above dry Africa, beasts from bad days,
squeaking like rubber, now radiant little suckers all.
I'll have to give it to those roaring theocrats:
angels may be antiseptic, but still they have orgies there,
perpetually in the blood-filled light, ah God.
I have reached my decision: this is the jump-off point.
Fix the struts, my helmet and chute. And now for to hang there...
only the wind, only air, only that consumption of haloes...
A light-weight answer to such a heavy question maybe,
but faced with such prejudice, I become just frivolous.
Come on, guys, raise funds in your own defence;
poets are meant only to raise spirits.

CHILDREN OF RA

Original title: The Economy of Nature
or, The Grand Hymn of Ra
attributed to Akhenaton, B.C. 1372
whose wife we know, Nefertiti
and son-in-law Tutankhamen,
the master of pharaonic glyphs
(freely translated from a version in French):
'How very numerous the things you have created
Even those deeply hidden from view
O Unique God above Whom is no other,
The universe you have created following your heart,
Remaining alone:
All things, men, herds and savage beasts,
All those on earth who walk on paws and feet,
Those who climb and may sail on their wings,
All of Egypt and its hinterland;
You have made each person in place and foreseen his needs,
Each to his nourishment, the length of his life counted,
Divided by languages of different expression,
Since you have cut us off from strangers
Our characters like our skins are distinct,
Remaining alone:
Cities, districts, fields, highways, rivers,
But you are the disk of day over the earth.'

For the Middle Dynasty this was a fine manoeuvre,
one Sun-God, monotheism for all,
the obviously superior lonely power
that made mud crawl, fruit seed,

such obvious glory to strike all living things;
post-empire stuff really, the union of the gods,
God is for a business-like religion and the pyramids
he had built with untold labour
on deserts in the plain light of day,
his arrogance to reach his God first,
King of Upper and Lower and all other Egypts,
Akhenaton the Heretic after whom
the lowly lapsed into rivalries anon.

MISADVENTURES

I

Nimrud ivory, VIII c. B.C.

A carved stone, paste and ivory plaquette,
the Assyrian dread of the Upper Nile;
fleshy lips, curly hair and da eyes wide...
In order to break the confederation of tribes
the royal lion-cub against an elegantly
executed background of river vegetation
readies himself, paw about the neck
to puncture the youth. Who falls backward
as if already dead, is held.

II

Antinopolis, 130 A.D.

Antinous (19), a slave, on a bend in the same river,
dived to save his gasping king, Hadrian (50),
tangled in red lotus, drowned, went down.
For such loyalty his lord, his liege,
built up this oozing outpost in His Name,
immortalised his body, curly lips,
his sturdy readiness to leap like a dog.

BATTLEPIECES

I
Italo-Abyssinian, 1895

When Menelik, Emperor of Ethiopia,
met the invaders at Adowa on March 1,
with more than 100000 modern rifles...
in short order the Imperials sacrificed:
56 cannons, 260 officers,
3000 of their own men, 2000 askaris
and 954 permanently missing.
At the Peace of October 26
the aggressors agreed to withdraw
their protection, to bury their bones
deeply in that arid gulch.

II
Turko-Italian, 1911

To evict in revenge the red janissaries
from rotten Tripoli they land:
reclaim the Roman ducts for water,
terraces for floating wheat. Unbowed,
their Arabs of the interregnum
(called Arabs, but they were an unknown tribe)
rebelled, were rounded up in the dunes.
Executed. Like hunters they pose
behind their pile of many-coloured fowl.

EPIGRAMS

I

The tsar's painter could fix his profile so:
'European' for a man of the New Style,
the voice of a nation, languid in exile,
but Pushkin preferred his 'Moorish look', said no.

II

Identified in a queue at a prison mess
an old grey lady with blue lips asked
if in poetry she could describe this last,
for her, scene... and Akhmatova answered yes.

SYMPOSIUM

'Therefore, Phaedrus, go back to that speech-writing
commander, whose word is the law in this place and whenever
he loves one can afford to pay with more than endearments;
I tell you there's no gain in an old and a young outcast
staring through the stream at their twenty toes;
refreshing in this heat to pass the time in lessons,
but usually you know I'm paid too for what I recommend... '

'Love is not for money; money is for other things.'

'I said, you know I'm paid too for my advice;
refreshing in this heat to pass the time in dialogue,
staring through his stream to find our twenty toes.
You cannot give my science the love it deserves.'

'You're beginning to repeat yourself; I said I want *your* love,
not his.'

   'I heard you the first time;
look at my wings, I have not seen yours sprout and uncurl.'

'You always talk in poetic devices; say what you mean.'

'Foot, blue veins, used blood, that what you want?
Your tender toes have never worn down stone.'

'He dandles me; he softens my slippers. I see your
big toe is up, the hairy patch, the rising moon.'

'I know, boy, stop this now.'

'And as the water
flows, so will I be a horny man and you be gone... '

Socr. to the youth, hand on knee: 'Look, tell him to cut
to the point: love is the highest god of all,
without whom men would not know what men
may be... and at his next law-giving he
should insert a pension for philosophers like me.'

C. V.

B. in a low outpost where the sun at last set,
1941 - in that Cape at war, sheltered pet;

adored in class, his hands entwined in prayer and others',
he learned books and to box, bagged adoring mothers;

adolescent left the Commonwealth and civilised sport,
for a third of a century roamed with a lousy passport;

educated in formidable skills and exacting in type,
this egregious gringo talked well, avoided hype;

now retired early to develop his pen, modestly pensioned...
before it's too late send all offers to the abovementioned,

in English and any compatible currency,
append photo and conditions of residency.

FOR WHOM I WRITE

When I'm asked by surprise not what poems I write
    but for what audience,
I stammer with awkwardness, as I do not believe those
    for whom I write to be that extensive,
and say with growing interest and conviction:

for the barber under whose hand my hair stands up to be cut,
for the reciped lady in the village who doesn't even understand
    my language, but feeds me her ice-cream nevertheless,
for the boatman who scuffles the soles of his black shoes
    before sliding the gangway on to the hydrofoil,
    signalling advance,
for the seller who studied too much, sees her fine baby
    swimming like two carp in her inch-thick lenses,
for some of the scholars and writers competing in deadlock here
    if they have a moment from deadlines and faxes,
and yes, for other poets whom annually I attend to
    but avoid for the rest of the year
    (our readers are too few, our acts to appealing
    for room for too many of those);

but not for the thieves who robbed and beat at the station
    innocent passengers travelling hopefully
    abroad for the first time,
nor the moony police too crooked to catch one of them,
not for the makers of bad movies, exorbitant needles, and those
    who feed their guernseys to fart a hole in the stratosphere,

those poets back home without humour who still use
                                        descriptions
   like 'rippled pink', 'rhythmical outpour' and 'swollen breast'
   without irony,
for whom irony is an essentially bourgeois phenomenon
   and self-irony only a sign of their guilty conscience,
for whom pleasures are deferred to heaven -
not for those do I write, as they wouldn't enjoy
   any of my travail, my effort, or understand its worth;

back to that barber now with his one day's growth,
   the middle finger on my crown tilting it in the mirror,
   studying me studying myself - now there is an artist
   at work, and I agree to respond to him, oh yes,
and the kind woman with the cone, spatula poised, advising,
   knows her worth,
etc. and so forth. For these, with them
   the poem comes to life.
The rest, absolutely not.

PASSAGES

While I was writing the below:

the soul of a racing driver flushed out of
      his red helmet on an S-bend
      like a speck of excrement;
the procession to the shrine on the cliff-edge
      reached the ruins of Spain
      tumbled over;
twice I stood, cleaned my nib,
      threw the scrap out, returned to the process.

There's no going back now.

My country finally for the first time
      in most of the people's memory
      changed its government
      to great applause, tears and thanksgiving,
which I have seen on TV
      with other events almost given up on:
      exhumed Jews, murdered children,
      bodies of partisans tumbled in ditches,
      the tribesmen in lakes and fridges
      or a speck under the palace floor.

While writing this I did hold back time,
      but could not stop or reverse it -
      in that sense life is not the news -
      and I have been bumped on to change;

and you have been changed too,
      reading the above.

CLEAN HANDS

Andreotti, but it could have been any of them,
Under the prosecutor's glare: at last, unprotected;

On archival footage once he sought out cameras,
Lied consistently into hand-held mikes: evidence against;

This one collected the drop when his guards where outside,
In a slick barbershop, while shaved with a cut-throat;

The revealing detail: he kept his famous glasses on,
Not as it turns out to check for nicks on the jugular,

But in respect for those square shoes under the curtain,
As it were, owned by his boss, dictating;

A nod, the briefcase full of cash pushed across -
Good family men these - pushed across for the confidence of a
                                                    nation;

Then back to parliament, the polls, clean-shaven - that's how low
The mighty have stooped, hands washed in the blood of lambs.

SOUTH TO SOUTH

Ai ai ai, the pampas and the great Karoo,
the rodeo in Montevideo and the grapes in the Cape,
the Great Kuiseb and the roaring River Plate,
you say the Atlantic between should be no obstacle,
by latitude we are sisters, right, after all,
and haven't we both just emerged from such family dishonour?
Ai ai ai, our ancestry and southern flare,
beneath all the posters and the platitudes,
settlers who fled wars and ought to depend no longer
on the great coat-racks of New York and Madrid,
we're connected bimonthly by Varig or SAA
from apartheid to Antarctica non-stop.
And look what we exchange for our mutual use: small arms,
bully-beef, interrogators, frozen deep-sea fish.
Ai ai ai, the tangos and the mangoes I can't miss;
I promise you I'll visit, on one condition:
you visit first.

AFRICAN SHAKE

This greeting - pads imprinted,
the swivel of thumbs, locked,
like hand-puppets, agreed - so
with deep contented sighs
gives time for more than recognition:
sights are lowered, bores uncocked,
aah yes... an African agreement.
Cannot be broken, comrade.
Don't ever forget or apologise.
More than symbolic, we are united.
Uh-hum. Until next time.
When I'm overseas I miss
those paddling palms. Pump air.

MY GARDEN

(*VOLTAIRE*, b. 1694)

My own garden I need to cultivate,
said Candide thanks to Voltaire,
hurt by his world, to defy it.

Mine I have likewise grown in state,
where droughtless and green it cleans the air
and the public may not deny it.

The private fuse of my country's hate
I thus convert, burning delight from despair,
free entry for those who won't buy it.

The bug-eyed bitch too pushes the gate,
sniffs the lawn and contributes her share,
here stones hold roots and only the flowers riot.

Build your own garden before it's too late,
speed the seed and the stem, the maidenhair,
squat in it, grow, don't be evicted.

Once Eve provoked Adam to fall for the bite
in that libellous tale of the sexist old snare,
but humankind came to belie it,

and now the serpent's gone to hibernate,
election's been declared free and fair,
paradise is recovered, come occupy it.

FIREFLIES

MY CHILDHOOD WAS LIT BY GLOW-WORMS - *Tanure Ojaide*
(1994)

I remember my childhood I thought with fireflies...
but I don't, there were not: none such;

nor the cherry-blossom, acacia-thorn blooming,
a fault in the mechanism, not those either;

some hay for fever, oranges for itchy bumps,
perhaps my body remembers only those deeply;

the rest is compensation for other people's poems,
for the blossoms the fruit, the flies the raging fire;

the limbs lag behind, bumped and spiky;
unseasonal the memory dies; only reputation's

left behind... these were organisms previously:
slow-burning, lush at night, must be believed in, recur.

CHILD AT LAKE COMO

The way the stick-child stands, elbows on the rail,
    one shoe on and one shoe off,
the baggy shorts, the flapping white shirt,
    shoulders pinched against skull
in a family photo facing the long grey lake

reveals some of his heritage: an Italian holiday
    beneath glaciers of grey snow,
the grooved Cisalpine slopes, divided
    by Caesar himself, the Romantic
mist over deep dark terraced ever-blue,

these busy villas which Pliny the Younger built
    to manage the local population,
easy; refined; quiet now as a crystal, watering-place
    beyond the war-like plains where Christ stopped:
for exiles and the over-taxed; their last resort.

His just post-Fascist Saturday in Nineteen Fifty;
    not that he could really comprehend it,
then the execution was no longer commented on,
    . nor the rusted axes in bundles
still declaring the ruined bomb-sites pestilent.

Yet to learn the impact of the firing-squad
    against any wall - his last mistress
flung across his chest to soften the lead -
    this revenge on a tinpot demon
whose awesome troops managed to cut through

whole multitudes... the evil of their policy,
    without respect for law, without love,
his own wrecking regime commencing only then:
    fascisti, naziskins, boers,
motors of horror, the ghastly cultural sideshow.

Before him, innocent, the forked lake extends
    like a long dowser's rod,
from a desert land his mitts have ticked,
    ticked down: here abundance,
the tug of divine water keeps enthralled.

Or the festive modes of locomotion
    like old steam engines fascinate,
means of boyish escape: a paddlesteamer,
    winded and leaky, shuffling
the swell with a flappy vapourish short temper.

His embarkation for no particular port:
    borne on tension like a lilypad,
shiny; shaken; the tied tongue slightly
    unknotted by the mechanical burr,
steaming into the sump of immense Alps...

Able to nod now, say: this is me, my name,
    a Proper Colonial Boy as planned,
no other direction but that chosen for him
    - idling into an education -
privileged to travel nowhere, first class.

The one question that may not be asked: had he known
    the betrayals to come, the sudden deaths,
the sell-outs and frauds and more, would he
    like anyone else have kept looking on,
grabbed in his hold what should have been avoided?

Do children's rights include what's always best
    for them: some portion of deck to stand on,
a real pull of affection and the being told where to go?
    When a holiday band played
marches and azaleas bloomed, he did step down.

I know if I now don't take pity on that mite,
    so thin he looks swollen headed,
knock-kneed, freckled in black-and-white;
    don't acknowledge and contain his little self,
I remain lost, I am over, I am incomplete.

His hand holds this pen: look where the nib
    leads you, it takes with a long, clean
line the poem and the continuity, the writing into
    what history was to do to him, what occurred,
he lived through too much... clenched; stopped.

Held there. On the postcard plate of a concertina
    Kodak, of pre-War quality,
a doting mother snapped for sibling and spouse.
    Look what he gets to experience here
he can't have over there, on the world's new edge.

So skinny bones, Skew Ears, this last remark:
    from now on we could do with a lot less
dreaminess, no more lounging, chewing cud;
    there's a whole lot of labour to undertake,
all of it needs to be learned and done!

There's a decent deal to be worked out as well,
    poets to undo and to correct -
these vengeful gangs, the class that is corrupt
    must be unbundled and demobilised -
with focus on the levee, before that brutal flood.

MARINA GRANDE

My mother and I - yes, another sentimental memory -
once visited the Island of Capri with its Tiberius' leap
(like Shaka's Rock), its Hotel Quisisana where
when Wilde entered to dine after his disgrace

other guests left, and Our Lady of the Blue Grotto
where pale or tanned or brown skin shines azure…
street arabs dehydrate, smoke cigarettes like Vesuvius
and at the Marina Grande: 'Ma, what is decadent mean?'

'Well, decadent, my boy… is something only poets do.'
'And gigolo?' 'That's different - any man can be those part-time.'
'Why do the Kaiser and Von Gloeden raise their eyes like saints
'and why must the local lads all wear those badges?'

Io non mi do on blue enamel (Myself I do not give).
'Well, diseases they may contract, unwanted habits.'
'You mean like begging, workless touts?' 'Not quite.'
'*What* then, when history promenades the sand and sin

like a suntan lotion wets the air, even Anglicans
perspire… here on the Marina Grande?' 'One day
you'll understand. Hold tight, there's a wave, a wave.'
That's how it was, nagging for the sheer pleasure, words

with much evasion until - *thwap,* the giggle-os,
the innuendos, nuzzles to look forward to, overwhelmed
in salt and tug, and a thousand decadent youths
flail hairily into the aftertow to rescue us.

HERITAGE DAY

A romance of hers in aid of Lions or Red Cross
besides our lake in for once a long Vaal spring -
unseated, a black lady has an oar jammed in barbed-wire;
howling down, the prehistoric hadedahs patrol -

so how do I remember her?, a boss-eyed Jewish sage
on another lake: Garda it was, Sirmione, then:
Miss J. smoking like a brazier, hacked at a portable
sagas that hardly showed the outlaw she was

and she said: *we will be free*: you: me: us: them:
write off that English death (puff puff) and *don't lie*
(here classical Catullus turned sparrow, entered his Lesbia,
forced at his villa's bath where girls used to play...)

less shocking for a child: if you go in front at lunch-time
all the flies are in the kitchen! *Tell true*, if not
at least laugh it off... penny per word, cased, pulp,
don't trust even print: only the bits of memory, dear.

SPRING

Trying to get a rise out of you,
Hopkins, your aspersion of holy dew;
tongue-in-cheek surely, your exuberant riffle,
poetry split on the rack of liturgical piffle;
getting the mouse out of the mick,
the occlusion of Lenten arithmetic;
three, four the petals of a clover
lead to gloryholes and supernova;
from winter's monochrome to the anaglyph
of Spring - O woken and risen stiff,
adolescent lambswool and dead men's bones,
the haycropper's bottle, spat cherry stones!
What *is* all this juice? asks the man,
aghast and unglued at His spray diagram;
his priestly wet dream under candlewick,
his incontinence, his unruly prick
like a goldfish gawping into weed,
the convulsion as at last he pukes his seed...
Poor Gerard Manley, unmanned by a Ghost,
for you I raise this driven toast:
for every saint, alas, the dingy satyrs,
for every bright martyr a hundred masturbators,
the sublime may sublimate the rustle
of season, its tissue, subdue its muscle,
the rest of us without being coy
find the prostate's clench our favoured joy.
So spring depends on what is sprung
in you, redolent and well-hung,

we no longer flock to the church,
we fuck when we get the urge.
We admire but will not kiss
the fiery kingfisher of the bugler's lips,
dappled with flame at his First Comm-
union, wafered by your hand, daubed dumb.
Pardon the frankness, dear Holy Roman -
speaks the Age of the Baby Bowman -
agape we welcome our fellatio,
more anus than agnus dei, you know.
But be honest, sir, bonded in sonnets,
tumbling and bursting with jets and vomits,
your rhythm, hey, rucked and stressed,
the scape of convention when broken is best blessed.
Could only be contained by the chaplet
of your strung, slung final riming couplet.

CONNECTIONS

I

My short lyric may no longer record -
in the first person, present tense,
confessing to you in the second -
the great message I wish it to,
thrown-up in the perfect old apercu;
sparse seems bare now, congested what was dense.
Instead of nailing to feeling there,
I wish to escape into a narrative run-on
tale and your prosy character sketch...
Ellipses are the stepping stones of your spine.
Across the order of my categories,
you lower yourself, fractious beast,
athwart my rime, taking a lot out
of me, disordering my former control.
Like a knout the thwap of your hand
is all that I'm left to understand:
that *colon* my closing *colophon.*
(Short lyric interrupted by activity.)

II

But to unman a muse another way:
twist and shake what you wish to say.
Don't make into mystery what everyone knows,
drop your old guard instead of clues,
what's contorted must be sorted, drop your load
instead of lies, give your word, that counts,
followed by tongue-hand-hip-haunch.
And before the whole almighty ravel gives,

60

for God sake learn to fucking split infinitives.
Here's what I am if you punctuate me:
"O" ....!!; enter again and be free.
(All of the italics are mine.*)*

III

(My turn.) Let's get down to the well-knit,
firmer than coy, finer than o-so-cute,
love is two words hyphenated, portmanteauxed,
the hairy root expressed in the hoary hole:
your eyes' diaeresis, the early grave-stress
of an elbow, the other lies acute,
the tilde of your hip, the pubic circumflex,
whoosh to the cedillas of your long tits,
fig. speaking... (the knobs of your spine again)...
an arse (vulg.) is an anus, inter-glutaei,
and would your derriere or posterior vent
by any other name smell as sweet?
This mount I know is heaven-sent.
These make for closer definition: verbs
kept regular, nouns proper, vowels open;
the genitive case: *ours.* Yours and mine.
We must complete our sentence, decline
each part and particle before we detumesce:
so unknot your shy pose, the ampersand
of our sweet embrace, your knees propped
round my bending neck, my line at last endstopped.

IV

Leaving my mouth free I may reflect
on the nomen nudum *of our rubberised act.*

The romans may be yours, mine the autonym;
your nonstandardised suffix and your dative case
you only use to Capitalise your smooth Shaft.
Just lower your parts of speech, you hasty glutton,
or else you'll come I declare on my belly-button.[1]

V

Milkman's on his round and so are we again,
the sniff of cream only makes one want more;
keep the cock in hand before conscience takes o'er,
ah! thought 'twas all a dream of a succulent snatch,
but now I have to learn it wasn't. Catch
as catch can, the early matutinal testosterone.
I'll quicken that up. *Toast, mate, and eggs:*
there's one crack, and another, frying on your legs,
I mean the non-stick pan, you tell me now:
scrambled like an anagram. Grass widower,
like the bird in nuptial plumage and long tail,
secondary characteristics. Signalling ambiguous.

VI

No double-meaning here. Take the bottle,
shake and shake. None'll come and then a lot'll.
Splash, courtesy Nash. What no curly bacon?
Is a veggie house. *Oh ja, the radish juice*
I suck from you is organic albumen,
so is your snot in the order of carrot puree,
your knob when it weeps weeps apple sap,

1. *Footnote*
Four of them with twenty toes like periwinkles,
Dreaming of drilling oysters for their ooze;
Or of the pedicure of tickled arches,
Horning into the softest socks and leather shoes.

I want more of it now, and when you bleed
I assure you your blood is not blood
but B12 and lecithin,
in your sperm are no cat-o'-nines
flailing the flood, but the pasteurised,
sterilised, radiated residue of gunk.

VII
Safe of course, our non-viral conjunction,
Coffee, white's, good for sexual function.

VIII
See ya tonight?

IX
Soonest.

X
Every night?

XI
Done.

DIALOGUES

I

Jean Cocteau
Mistrust good reviews, find cupid stupid,
let the pen on the page be your best release;
avoid all women who praise your facile youth,
I lock you indoors till you're a masterpiece.

Raymond Radiguet (banging on the wall)
For you fame is the spurt, the needle of desire,
the genius show; for me only secular is sexual,
the penis my nib and if I wish to reproduce
my ink I'll squirt singly, be individual.

Cocteau
Stroke, stroke, take the bastards by storm,
prodigies must prove prodigious.

Radiguet
I'll overcome them one by one, cock in the hole,
your rigid rod, oh I fall, faint - is too rigorous.

Cocteau
Subdued, get a grip on yourself, repent!

Radiguet (sinking to the floor)
I do. I dictate the perfect sentence.

II

Beatrice Hastings
My cheeks I pinch to make myself blush,
after the intrusions of Zeppelins and Sigmund Freud,

there's no shame left to uncover - your brush in my tush -
we'll all be destroyed by unequal loves, be destroyed;
which will get you first, TB or the trenches,
having to sit and sit for you gets lonely,
your risen hood, my clench and drenches,
and all I want is some conversazione.

Amedeo Modigliani
These colonial bitches have no shame, none.
They'll take up any pose, complain, complain,

Hastings
Painting me for love, the routine of Bohemia,
strokes, strokes: seamier, steamier.

Modigliani
Humph. Nearly finished... Done. Done. Now...

Hastings
It's all over then. Let me harden, let me dry. Ciao...

    III

Radiguet
Only *une Africaine* may save Modern Art,
we knot and coil the continents, headstrong heart and soul,
don't tell Modi, don't tell Jean... apart
from you no circuit, periphery to metropole.

Hastings
Tula, bambino, tula at my beaten breast,
for this one truly gives up all the rest...
Dust we'll have in hand, no immortality,
the curly stand of flesh convinced... sh, sh.
(The bombardment proceeds.)

BILLETS-DOUX

To Verlaine

On all fours in that gaslit b + b,
Brutal British to teach our skilful tongue;
Lick my arse, stuprous, *lick-spittle,* you and me;
The carnation (write it) blooms, gurgle and come;

You adore me, cored me, parlezed to Jack and Joy;
Your risen cock combed (write) my nutty prostate,
This aischrologia: *fucked, fucked,* underage boy...
Finger-love, lip-hate, we bless - I mean *wound* - copulate.

Vent (.), adventure (o), hypervent (o), hole (O),
Tradesmen only, workers join one another, hold (   );
Ah, your receding forehead and crumpled horn milked,

The hairy, streaky violet (write it down): older sods
Are imprisoned for broken syntax, pricks and prods,
So enclose me (now), before I fall... I am filled.

To Rimbaud

To that kid marooned at the Cape of Storms, runaway,
This private missive (at least you have some Engleesh,
Amid the Dutch aux Colonies and dirty trade;
They make a good stiff pontac, but do they have speech?):

Alors, mon brave... yes, it's bad without you, wrecked.
Protégés I've had, hopeless, they won't engage,
Don't find the dialogue; so soldier erect,
Bring your scar back, your stump, to love's come-of-age.

Or do you, my correspondent, need now to blast and blunt
The dark herbal in turn, our patrilineal hunt?
Recollect that star (.) burst (*), burnt archipelago,

The sticky, prickly heat of our sombre metrification,
The pride of pâté-ing our meat-headed, stuffy nation:
This envoi as you're inscribed, before you rise up and go.

THE BARON SALUTES THE WORKERS

Salve, ragazzi. In iam-5 and terza rima
(grand plan) I recall Venetian days, raw and oversexed,
when the first was dark-eyed Arno the schemer,

who ran like a red river through all my great text
of the black world, was written out, with a finger reinserted,
I fully satisfied myself he was addressed and undressed;

and Benjamin the unhooded younger, who flirted
first in the piazza, the portal, whose limbs enjamb-
ment splayed mine, who at the sight still stood and spurted;

Dan the dopey apprentice punter, what haunch and ham,
son of my keeper who hates each and every pederast,
poles this barcarole, lamb's blood, blood of the lamb;

'Such a lovely figure - Ennio - muscular, rosy' (iconoclast),
'carrying sacks he was down a plank, the peachy part
'sprayed with lily-flower' (beauty your dermoblast);

those days soap-makers, hands and honey, another tart
included Federico, my own real name in foliate:
specular, his lips on broken glass, slightly broken heart;

(we know) 'poor boys may be sucked for a cigarette'...
the stormwashed lagoon, this rime a daisy-chain
of lances and lunges - poor flickering, creamed expatriate!

But then came Ugo, little Ugo, whose Milky Lane
said Drink, drained himself dry, whose pizzle
stirred this beef; after such pleasure, such pain!

Gabriele I neglect, my dog, his prickly muzzle,
wing-beaten guardian, crush of soft lavender
after such loud laundering, the faint gentle drizzle;

and Giacomo sweet, monicker for James, first offender,
the riddle of whose sphincter turned a prison to stone,
his kingly perversion spent in the arms of big spender;

Luca his folly, but why Luca the paper clone,
when Ugo - Ugolino - was available, the last trump
in his breeches summoning kneelers, worshippers prone,

O Ugo, most cruelly abused, whose woven stump
woke a neighbourhood and woke again the pealing tower,
shook the tidal wave, the root in the rump,

the parting of his hair like wheat, his belly too, sweetly sour,
so mournful! (this is becoming Rilke at Duino)
who when he flew... took all my dotage, my dower,

who lost a molar, spat Coca-Cola, whose macho
nailbitten digits down to half-moons eclipse,
whose, whose, whose... absence... is the brunt of my discordo.

Luca and Marco the evangels, and Paulo who strips
in the sheds, lets tourers grope through linen his rod,
the scaffolding his outdoor theatre, tilts his hips -

even cardinals revert to rut, that plasterer, carries hod,
washes their walls white, preaches lick and spit,
great manual seducer! But Ugo brought me closer to God.

Dante dropped all sods in a Grand Canal of shit,
a comedy turn for coprophage, squitter and lickarse;
my surfers today wear suits against sewage; the orchid

of his last vent is my pry and my make mass,
my enter-and-be-damned, my punishment for no real crime;
the engorgement of these things will all come to pass.

Puff the bumf, Rorschach test of the sublime:
a cleft blot, my signature. Nobly piled and varicose.
You become this last note, given time, given time.

So what do you have for me today? - hold me hard, close -
Dachau, all concentrated camp for sad old queens?
Koffiefontein for moffies, ovens for gingerbread, a light dose

of gas in the Turkish bath where old has-beens,
massaged and spanked, like to recollect and be wanked;
the cadets inhale and pop, cyanide ethnically cleans.

And the prospect of a tip of nudes, heaven be thanked,
members rigored with bacteria - my man, the worm -
under a lawn with no herm or monument, no crosses ranked.

What else do you have on your list? Jewish sperm
and Gypsies', too - God gave them enough, I should know;
sterilise; abort each sucking foetus before term.

I append for you like loins on a pelvis a last show:
Rocco the mediator, the charm, who works off his rocks,
his cherry-ripe, catches in one celestial blow

all epidemic outbursts of the pest and the pox,
the acqua alta of my amorcord (but one), (my tongue
's my weapon) (in cheek, his) - Vitellino in socks

(bow legged). Line up and salute, my hung
and raunchy gondoliers, A to Z, X for your choice:
slang (unzip a word: woe, woe) and slung;

only one we miss, but as through a nostril a cloud... a voice,
the OO of his golden glasses, the pouted lip below,
those tingle-tangle testes, rejoice yes rejoice!

This one, brought back, his burning guts, his sweaty flow,
his sad cypress lets me be languidly laid,
his handful is all you know, and all you need to know.

And they were jealous and despaired, touched him and were afraid!
Beneath his pubic punkah rests the sturdy magistrate,
the jury for support, their judgment to be made:

sentenced to lashes and bars, to wear forever straight
laces, to have no humour or perspire hormones or hurt,
to miss a beat, be mistaken, beaten, early or too late,

to rouge the valves and vacuums, filiate and flirt,
tread the treddle of a diaphragm, breast for open sea,
eat ashes, cry salt, to grovel in the continental dirt.

Headland and promontory, way-station, my apogee...
ah my lad with rasped, chewed thumbs, beyond their lex-
icology... dead and done, well... what will be, will be...

Still at night I hold your hand, cup your sleeping sex,
have irrefragable fantasies that you, sodden dreamer,
your labour and buxom has ended. These reamer's tercets

are your viaticum. *Vale*, my friend. Concludes my schema.

THE MARTYRDOM OF SAINT SEBASTIAN

Acupuncture, he suggests, these arrows piercing
the limbs to the bole of the tree,
though the rictus of the lips, the bulging eye
suggests no cure - only deep all-over pain,
a thorough dread, holding back the last gasp.
Mantegna best catches this new kind of torso.
I have the old on my wall, Knabenstatue Nr 698,
an ephebe unblemished, with a faint
sniff in the nostrils, garlanded innocent,
who in the house raises his growing arm in salute.
This one's own platoon turned on him,
used his belly for target practice,
as in empire days they aimed at savages.
O archers, archers, shed your purple togas for Christ!
An icon to lure the fond gaze on high,
remind the flesh what it takes to be subdued.
These arrowheads nick, tear; the shafts plunge,
the feathered butts whistle as he takes
the impact, takes again the thwarted,
jabbed desire to hold on... the scrim
about his waist like a billowing dhoti -
all that's left of his kit, shaps
and leather breastplate - soaking in his blood
and piss... *O Lord, how can I hold?*
The sadistic fresco pins him there
without deposition, his story arrested,
Christ's poorly porcupine. Faith
was the message: intravenous blades forcing

in the iron-age drip of agony.
But still I hear: *Lord, can I hold?*
Who can bear, who can bear,
when they're only mortal and have no soul?
Ah Lord, fold me now and let me die,
millions will suffer and never know why,
do not make martyrs popular or an excuse,
hold my hand now, wipe my brow -
Sebastian of Gaul, captain under Diocletian,
d. in Rome, c. 288 Anno Domini.

GÉRICAULT'S SHIPWRECK

Before classically he had done the portraits of fine mares
    Held in meadows, flowergirls, Napoleon's feathers;
But then news of an uneasy scandal, legally suppressed,
    Exposed by journalists, human muck washed in;
Three hundred low citizens lost when not one need have been,
    And the captain by Louis restored… got only three years;
Two in the making the canvas for which Paris and London queued
    Had the Governor (Schmaltz his name) at last recalled
From Senegal with his cargo of Gambian gum and cotton; cheap
                                                        cotton.

    For this propaganda piece the painter changed his way
And in the end, his red locks shaven, sacrificed even his life;
    At what he found he went insane - men ingesting down
Their own waste, their water, one another: meat.
    Uncovered his own country's necrophile state: the poverty
Of a beaten kingdom, bad Paris, plague, demented at last.
    An awful death, tugged in the stirrup of his mount.
For the Salon of 1819 this monstrous raft all knew about
    Had to be admitted. Title: 'Scene of Shipwreck' -
The livid panorama of the exposé of the log of the disgrace,
    The survivors themselves recognisable therein;
The erotics of hope, that rush of suppressed narrative
    The censor may not always stop: the truly, utterly appalling.
First note the absence: no Marianne in this glazed, stripped bustle
    Breasting the flood in frank, financial gauze.
Rather these are her colonists: branded convicts, veterans of
                                                        Waterloo
    Under what Henze at least calls a 'black sun' and Barnes

Agrees are fatal conditions: time exonerates injustice
    He wishes; but the point is art should not, ever:
Nor does the sea's cruelty excuse bloody fraternal inefficiency;
    Like so much else, he sees no negroes there as indictment -
But four are clearly in view, their confessions and their bodies
    Of bitumen too raw for even the English to champion;
Rollers should swallow, ragged teeth clench, breakers enfold,
                              disperse.

    Starring Jean-Charles as the pyramid's pride,
From a model sharing his dish: strip, reach, stretch, wave rags -
    Their mascot - sinking on their bony shoulders as...
Their rescuer sails on - the speck most studied in Western
                          perspective -
    And this is his unstopped story dictated in pain:
'I, Jean-Charles, slave, am manumitted from my chains
    By my old Good Emperor... by my new Bad King
I, Jean-Charles, because now I need payment cannot find work:
    Expelled like others of my "Afflicted Race"'
(The phrase is Wordsworth's who admired their 'tropic fire')...
    'I, Jean-Charles, as I am unemployed, am sent from my
                          motherland
In whose pastures I posed the buffed stud in his martingale
    (For M. Géricault no less), wore a hat of feathers too,
Walked the vendeuses in their and my pinpoint embroidery,
                        heard opera;
    A groom of such class, loving and loyal... am now banished;
Light and adroit so they hoist me... their Toussaint, their bright boy,
    And they have become my (forbidden word) - my camarades.

At the settlement of Saint-Louis in Africa, where I had never set
>> foot,
> My task was to be teaching other blacks to comport like me,
Sufficient numbers and alphabet, how to reap and not retain their
>> crop;
> Thus at the fringe would I perpetuate what the metropole
>> forbids,
Where may enjoy the capital none but the fruits of its hypocrisy.'
> (This moral Wordsworth, Henze and of course Barnes miss...)
'But young Jean-Louis-André-Theodore, called Géricault,
> As he explains to me once and for all as I strain, reach, freeze,
Intends to show them.' Soon died of exposure ashore...
> And here the limit of art must be: for verisimilitude
This painter studied fresh cadavers, stole rotten limbs:
> The nude of the dead lad sliding into gilt
Lay this way draped on the slab, groaning back... starved;
> In case he himself forgot he even placed aboard his replica
Fiery young Delacroix, further to advance this new, committed
>> programme;
> And thus he stacked an unimaginable tilted rush
- A salver of those cast-off - discharged into the deep;
> The abandoned, drawn from life, breaking frame,
>> unforgettable.
'O brothers in law' (the message should be) 'if you can't eat cake
> Eat shit... suitable deaths of hunks on such perilous hulks
Keep all ranks insecure, o liberty! o ineffable disaster!
> Lick the heaving turds from between my cheeks, ah!
My head I laugh off: divide and devour, abolish all famine,
> My only friend!' (quote from His Majesty at the private
>> showing).

Méduse... the rusty jelly sucks at, serpents strike at,
    Stone stares... a raft of untying fretwork, flotsam
For the whole Atlantic to gorge, as it has engorged millions,
    And not to enclose again without records kept.

OVID IN HIS EXILE

To polish the bright sun of Caesar's great patronage
   Blacken I must the little light of these, his others:
Make dumb the dour peasants, deny their utterances
   Have sane or subtle meaning, *bar bar bar*
Like their sheep or worse: wolves at this last Pontic gulch,
   Shaggy and snaggletoothed, these my ever-tender friends.
For Caesar I'll freeze, muddy, libel and once
   That fails coldly curse: plain savages, their not very
Poisoned arrows stuck in thatch like porcupines,
   Untamed their whooping cousins crossing
The Danube, or call it the Kei, into this Colony,
   Rooted on horses in warpaint, they raid and we lickety run...
Four-legged men so agile we thought exist only in myth.
   To whom we represent... well, this fearsome Rome.
Tomis, on the edge of the map of the known, beyond, over,
   Where if the sun will shine it shines
Every second season, but then I admit cosily enough,
   Browning the rising maize, our hair and hide,
While others' in their potency are turned gold and gilt.
   The Latin word is inscribed here without meaning:
They utterly lack all literacy. Yet will I never master
   Their oral techniques which put our regular poets to shame.
These primitives mean more than they say when at last they say it:
   They certainly fear Caesar, they do tell me they tremble;
To propitiate him they make this exception, they coddle me
                    along...

   When I die in their midst if he forgets me

How they'll keen over my mound in ragged, shaken syllables
    Of ice and fang and the recurring murrain,
Not recorded yet in script, too late ever to be left intact,
    No tombstone for me carved out longer than memory.
My poor lost bones, unfaithful epitome, they'll hug and howl at
    When they've drawn my breath, sucked my poor curse dry.
These are the Thracians who tore young Orpheus apart,
    Their previous poor poet; the relics they keep of him
To recant are his nimble fingers, his scrotal sac tied with a string -
    The streams in the unclaimed waste where they wash these
Glitter secretly for their own canny preservation:
    No forced labour yet here, only trade by the grain;
One of Caesar's passing legions, armour against black bristles,
    Should slash them, bring to heel, shoo them in,
A company for me to share and civilise, ransack my dears,
    A magistrate to construe and scan their resistance.
Metal for him, who as his emissary I tell them, loves, truly loves:
    Both ways poets deceive. In truth on the frontier
We all have this uncommon fear of falling off, cling;
    Power is awesome, but what those who have none
Admire is power that is wary of them, even their last independence.
    To these near-citizens I attach myself perforce with propaganda:
Their clannish house-calls I'll describe as martial abattoirs,
    Their gauche yearnings call only hunger and thirst,
Brutes, I will claim, they are devoid of beauty, naturally base,
    Her breast that plugs the dead cold with gnummy-yums
I'll call 'that uberous dugg' she slings twixt her own thighs,
    Heathen and unholy her prancing, beaded youths who
Mix semen and spew to brood and breed their wretched kine.

While others translate me, rehearse my cocked positions,
Switch the old plot for pleasure, here there is *no change;*
   As I am relegated I rail… dark, dark, dark.
Therefore they are ugly - *not mine* - though they tug me, take me,
   Clean me up once I've done with my fit,
Retch the alphabet, my skill, my unfair punishment, my loathing.
   From their midst, O Caesar, see how reduced I am:
Unconformable, without hope, utterly and friendlessly degraded…
   Without your mercy we share only the same shadow;
I thrust them from me: their commensality, my disgrace,
   I cast them off as you do me, and I vilify
These dirty-nailed fellows whom to my advantage I betray:
   Great Caesar's all, from whom we are all banished.

DEAD MAN'S DISCLOSURE

My soul to keep in a coffin, trod beneath (bare) (foot) people
    (my mortal remains), sloth-bear pads, goats graze
(pressed in wood) roots entwine (casket) (cask)

this where banyans walk in Muybridge locomotion
    reco(r)ding their raiders' myths of succession:
Taprobana Insula (Ptolemy) for Roman turtleshell
    Serendib for silk, Kandy for ruby
Copra from Ceylon, Beira (Slave Island) Lake

from rank mud ((lotus unfolds, their long Buddha
    (1) in meditation (2) in blessing (3) robed to recline,
like elephant skulls, from paddies, freckled hills arise,
    (moo) moonstone: fortunes picked in
broken orange pekoe (A1) fannings, plantations

(rimed recipes) (sun) stored in fruit: brinjal
    I did know, (papaya) (tobacco): not toddy-tappers
cinnamon-peelers, jaggery-makers (low classes in their *Gazetteer*).
    Down Aloe Vera Avenue, Armour Street
Britons speedy where Britishers meet: plant

rain-trees and bo-trees (Boer): (Anglo-Boer) war-time
    (prisoner). From my fever-ridden body grows,
saffron and sage… capsicum of chilli… and pepper, clove…
    cocoa, coriander, vanilla, mustard… ginger… gin
from my body: (star sapphire) (blue) (((pearl)))
    - the *Phoenix* and her fraught - cargoed
anti-clockwise from the Cape, this British lake
    between monsoons, between the Indian and the Bay of Bengal.

So I was captured in fair battle, once turned-about,
    beyond Pretoria (in chains)… like coolies
)*take me back*(enclosed in (Diyatalawa)
    (Mount Lavinia) (Ragama - hard labour)
(Urugasmanhandiya): mean death, we die like flies…

Some do escape… through birdsnest and staghorn,
    like a white-eye, sunbird, flycatcher, roller,
kingfisher, bee-eater, lorikeet, minivet, grackle
    (canary)… the long, slow sleek fish-eagle
swoops its prey from the shine of an artificial tank…
    where today a pilgrim shampoos his Yamaha
flops like a buffalo, his sarong a bandage unwinds

(Some died: I was one of the first and quickest to go):
    Kanattha Cemetery, among those gracious Dutch Burghers,
Anglican Section… on LP gas their cremation takes 2 hrs.
    (I'd have preferred ash)… where keepers with matchets
under Oriental weeping-willows under umbrellas hack flame-
    lilies from our disregarded tombs.
The jumbled roll-call of the dead and dying (in any order):

Leon Kock, Kruger, Joubert, Massyn, Smuts, Scott,
    Opgericht ten Gedagtenis aan…
Nel, Foley, Uys, Eckhardt, Kachelhoffer, van Biljoen,
    Rust in Vrede, Overl. te Selon (all present),
Oud 20 Jaar… An only son from a Household Gone,
    A Voice we Loved is Still, A Place
is Vacant in our Home, That Never Can be Filled.

Take me back to my renegade home… all we had to show
    (in the Colombo Museum, oil on canvas):
foreground, a commando with watering-can pours into a sloot,
    me in my smasher-hat with pipe, foot against the wire,
the sentry box… rows of military tents on the ridge
    where a mighty strangler-fig (holds)… (artist unknown).
Whippy king coconuts lift, majors with swords trepan.

Among contesting Lion People, Tiger people, at night mosquito coils,
    I lie so restless… drilled by croton, would like to learn to
treddle a sewing-machine, palm-paddle waylaying touts,
    like cows chewing newsprint begin to speak,
say: *Take me back to the Old Transvaal,* say:
    Honeymoon Hairstyle, sup at All Night Restaurant,
shave and dress in robes over a shoulder, scratch my Dreamland,
    sing the Sweet and Sour Serenade, find lost addresses:
Perera, Ferera, de Silva, Hulftsdorp, Graylands,
    fling at the devil firecrackers… Drive Him Off… Greet
the dog-faced Andaman as a friend. Those I would liked to have done.

But the order of procession is declared: I am no longer part,
    daar waar… my mother weeps and dies alone…
and awful death is no escape, from this lonesome (cell)
    (tibia) (socket) (jawbone) (dust)
(unto dust) I had hoped… remote past tense, done…
    her only support, her soul to keep in the rule of the gun.
Peace I would have made, justice practised, loved and bred.

I had hoped we could overcome the metal barb, the nameless trench…
    soldiers dig graves to dump in… their duty undertaken

I'd planned on amnesty... But now the slaughter's even worse, I hear.
 Better out of it, they say, better dead. So it's not fit
to live in, so join me here. (Join me.) Once, like you,
 I was all young blood and hopeful vision... Now:
disconnected calcium (homesick) (rotting) (spiritless):
 stripped even of metaphor and syllables, ah-ha...
a song like a T sunk in my unravelling lung...

(I. m. Ferrar Reginald Mostyn Cleaver,
State Prosecutor of the Witwatersrand,
d. 18 November, 1900, aged 30)

I. m. OLGA KIRSCH
(d. July 1997)

You took us through thickets in your desert,
drying orchards - frozen thorns, sapless -

a land short of water can no longer afford,
quoting in hearty Afrikaans, English and even old Hebrew

the hate-speech on the phone you had to field
as you frankly spoke out: *there are no lines*

between people, your God and mine made none:
in either of your countries, difficult poetry.

Israel without oranges - that sacrifice of the good,
the golden - is like South Africa without your voice.

GABRIEL'S EXHIBITION

What's a nice Jewish boy? Diamonds cut capture light.
Goldstar, Maccabee beer. Desert water into dust.
Gabriel, heavenly magister. Lavender and sage alert.
Limestone again, crannies. *Doing in a place like this?*

Bearer of compacts, close to God. Descends the blazing blue.
What's an archangel? Levant and couchant,
Solar warming the glory. Cannas and vygies bloom.
Doing in a place like this? The loaded loquats, the dates.

People of the Book and Plenty. A place like Nazareth.
Scarps and fountains, tamarisk. Silos and wells
Leak the cool grace beneath a barren, beaten earth.
Angel of dark sentences delivers in a cave the syllables.

Verbum Caro Factum Est. Saline Palestine brought to ruin,
Sodom and Gomorrah to salt. The end-of-khamsin Lake of Fire.
Silk and spices cross the trades. Begin to bloom, begin now to bloom
Their Fields of blood, their Hospice of new, unholy Desire.

And Mary the Carrier, the Egg-machine. *What was she?*
Climate for blood-stained glass. *Doing in a place like that?*
Heaven her only compensation. Her dangerous gynaecology.
Vale of Sharon, of Tears. Greet God's tower, his minaret.

Fishers of Kinneret. Olive and orange and oleander.
Pecan, peanut, nut brown, curling cashew and fig.
What's a, what's a? Also meet: Boaz and Emmanuel,
Tour guides. *Doing in a place?* So undelivered, so gagged.

Helicopter in the rain. This fin de millenaire.
Freighted with taxes to pay. In Bethlehem, in Jerusalem.
Conjure water into wine. aloC-acoC dna grebslraC.
Vino dell' Ultima Cena. *In a place* we all condemn.

Holly and thistle talk of pain, harp and cymbal of joy.
Story-maker Christ came to pass, was beaten, betrayed.
Know that Herod's barefoot warriors killed girl and boy.
Circumcised by the sword, in others' blood arrayed.

Was he so nice? And the Angel Gabriel lifted
Holy Muhammad too, in this polished stone his finger-marks.
Unredeemable place of rubble, truly God-forsaken, giftless.
Scab and palsy. Unclean. Lunatic and demoniac.

Like migrant storks, exiles return. Winged messengers.
Poison them. Have we learnt nothing at all? Big-eyed
Black saints from the Land of Cush arrive transgressively,
Blink at the splayed men, cringe before Kingdom Come,

Where down deep Wells of Souls only the dead pray for the dead.
And dear Righteous Honoured Gentiles share their diaspora,
As the mighty never are put down, nor raised those of low degree.
Nice womb-leaping babes never stop the war, the intifada.

Vision's to be interpreted, this belt of hell, this Israel.
Glad tidings of great distress. *What is a, was a, had been, went?*
Condoms three shekels. These notes stuck in the Wailing Wall.
Oil my palm. Mosque like a planetarium. Never heaven-sent.

Ten per cent off on crucifixes. *Et Habitavit in Nobis.*
Pizza, pitta, I don't see it, this is His body, my bread?
A nice Jewish… Never mind, cellphone to Yes, sir…
Feathery tumult, *this place,* I tell you, I dine with the done.

Golden I had hoped for, not such heavenly random, such arid rift.
Learn from this temple show, this tourist crossing, this fake position.
You're on your own, he won't come (radiant and golden and unspilt),
Annunciating saviours like water, like taste. Like nuclear fission.

Nor, unless your struggle-swords are beaten soon to peace-shares,
Your enclaves into echoes, dollars into dust, dust into fertile ash,
Will this bird-being, having words with mild Mary
Be heard out loud, as their bargain, their benediction is struck.

NOTES

'The Trojan Horse'

a reworking of a poem by William Drummond of
Hawthornden (1620).

'Poppies'

Written for the Wilfred Owen Association, using the stan-
dard image of the buttonhole of a red poppy to commemo-
rate the dead of the First World War.

'The Anna Mary Letters'

These four poems are closely based on actual letters by
Anna Mary, the last surviving member of the immediate
Livingstone family. They are preserved and exhibited in
the David Livingstone Centre at the Scottish National
Memorial at Blantyre, near Glasgow. Hans Christian
Andersen, the Danish author of fairy tales like 'The Little
Mermaid' and 'The Ugly Duckling', faithfully replied to
his growing young correspondent until his death in 1875.

'Slaughtered Saints'

The title is quoted from John Milton's sonnet, 'On the Late
Massacre in Piedmont' (1655).

'Nenuphar'

A rough reworking of Flavien Ranaivo's 'Prémices' (1962).

'Children of Ra'

The quoted central section is a translation of a version of the
original hieroglyphics by Théophile Obenga in French,
reproduced in *Présence Africaine*, Nos. 149-150 (Jan.-June,
1985).

'Heritage Day'

24 September in the new South Africa. 'Miss J.' is Naomi Jacob.

'The Baron Salutes the Workers'

The baron in question is Frederick Rolfe (1860-1913), whose *Venice Letters* are quoted. The form is Dante's canto.

'Géricault's Shipwreck'

Theodore Géricault (1791-1824), the early French romantic, first exhibited his painting 'The Raft of the *Medusa*' in 1819. It now hangs in the Louvre. The canvas depicts the situation of the castaways of the scandalous shipwreck of three years before, when the frigate-transport was stranded off the coast of Senegal as part of a convoy en route to the settlement of Saint-Louis, without any safety precautions having been taken. The king referred to is Louis XVIII of the Bourbon restoration. In 1802 William Wordsworth had dedicated a sonnet to Toussaint l'Ouverture, the Haitian revolutionary, and protested the expulsion of freed African slaves from Napoleon's France. Hans Werner Henze wrote an oratorio based on the Géricault painting in 1969, dedicated to Che Guevara. Julian Barnes devoted a chapter of his novel, *A History of the World in 10 ½ Chapters*, to the story of the painting in 1989.

'Ovid in his Exile'

Publius Ovidius Naso, the Roman court poet, was banished by Emperor Augustus to Tomis (Constanza) on the Black Sea amongst the gentle Thracians and, railing against his fate, died there in exile. An inspiration for this poem was Noël Mostert's history, *Frontiers* of 1992, which describes the process by which the Cape border district was colonised.